50 Meal Prep Recipes for Home

By: Kelly Johnson

Table of Contents

- Grilled Chicken and Quinoa Bowls
- Turkey and Veggie Stuffed Peppers
- Baked Salmon with Asparagus
- Chickpea Salad with Feta and Spinach
- Teriyaki Chicken Stir-Fry
- Mediterranean Couscous Salad
- Beef and Broccoli Stir-Fry
- Shrimp Tacos with Cabbage Slaw
- Sweet Potato and Black Bean Bowls
- Greek Chicken with Tzatziki Sauce
- Zucchini Noodles with Pesto Chicken
- Lentil and Vegetable Soup
- Egg Muffins with Spinach and Cheese
- BBQ Pulled Pork with Coleslaw
- Asian Peanut Chicken Salad
- Cauliflower Fried Rice
- Spicy Chickpea and Quinoa Bowl
- Lemon Herb Roasted Chicken Thighs
- Taco Meal Prep with Ground Beef
- Grilled Veggie and Hummus Wraps
- Overnight Oats with Berries and Almonds
- Curried Chicken Salad with Apples
- Spinach and Feta Stuffed Chicken
- Meatballs with Zucchini Noodles
- Quinoa and Black Bean Burrito Bowls
- Beef and Sweet Potato Skillet
- Caprese Pasta Salad
- Chickpea and Spinach Stew
- Grilled Shrimp with Mango Salsa
- Chicken Fajita Meal Prep Bowls

- Sweet and Spicy Chicken Drumsticks
- Baked Tilapia with Lemon and Herbs
- Ratatouille with Quinoa
- Thai Red Curry with Vegetables
- Greek Turkey Burgers with Tzatziki
- Pesto Chicken and Veggie Skewers
- Miso-Glazed Eggplant
- Creamy Tuscan Chicken
- Breakfast Burrito Bowls
- Black Bean and Corn Salad
- Roasted Vegetable and Quinoa Salad
- Chicken Alfredo with Broccoli
- Teriyaki Tofu with Mixed Vegetables
- Pasta Primavera with Chicken
- Lemon Garlic Shrimp with Broccoli
- Caprese Stuffed Portobello Mushrooms
- Chili Lime Grilled Chicken
- Vegetable Stir-Fry with Brown Rice
- Baked Ziti with Spinach and Ricotta
- Spaghetti Squash with Turkey Meat Sauce

Grilled Chicken and Quinoa Bowls

Ingredients:

- 2 boneless chicken breasts
- 1 cup quinoa, rinsed
- 2 cups chicken broth (or water)
- 1 bell pepper, diced
- 1 cucumber, diced
- 1 avocado, sliced
- 1/4 cup fresh parsley, chopped
- 2 tablespoons olive oil
- Juice of 1 lemon
- Salt and pepper to taste

Instructions:

1. Season the chicken breasts with salt and pepper. Grill over medium heat for about 6-7 minutes per side until cooked through. Let rest, then slice.
2. In a saucepan, combine quinoa and chicken broth. Bring to a boil, then reduce heat to low, cover, and simmer for 15 minutes or until liquid is absorbed. Fluff with a fork.
3. In a large bowl, combine quinoa, bell pepper, cucumber, and parsley. Drizzle with olive oil and lemon juice, then season with salt and pepper.
4. To serve, divide the quinoa mixture into bowls, top with grilled chicken slices, and add avocado.

Turkey and Veggie Stuffed Peppers

Ingredients:

- 4 large bell peppers (any color)
- 1 pound ground turkey
- 1 cup cooked rice (brown or white)
- 1 zucchini, diced
- 1 cup corn (fresh or frozen)
- 1 cup diced tomatoes (canned or fresh)
- 1 teaspoon Italian seasoning
- Salt and pepper to taste
- 1 cup shredded cheese (optional)

Instructions:

1. Preheat the oven to 375°F (190°C).
2. Cut the tops off the bell peppers and remove the seeds. Place peppers in a baking dish.
3. In a skillet, cook ground turkey over medium heat until browned. Add zucchini, corn, tomatoes, Italian seasoning, salt, and pepper, cooking for an additional 5 minutes.
4. Stir in cooked rice until well combined.
5. Fill each pepper with the turkey mixture and top with cheese if desired.
6. Cover with foil and bake for 30 minutes. Remove foil and bake for an additional 10 minutes until the peppers are tender.

Baked Salmon with Asparagus

Ingredients:

- 4 salmon fillets
- 1 bunch asparagus, trimmed
- 2 tablespoons olive oil
- 2 tablespoons lemon juice
- 3 cloves garlic, minced
- Salt and pepper to taste
- Lemon slices for garnish

Instructions:

1. Preheat the oven to 400°F (200°C).
2. On a baking sheet, place salmon fillets and asparagus. Drizzle with olive oil and lemon juice, then sprinkle with minced garlic, salt, and pepper.
3. Bake for 12-15 minutes or until the salmon is cooked through and flakes easily with a fork.
4. Serve garnished with lemon slices.

Chickpea Salad with Feta and Spinach

Ingredients:

- 1 can (15 oz) chickpeas, drained and rinsed
- 2 cups fresh spinach, chopped
- 1/2 cup feta cheese, crumbled
- 1/2 red onion, diced
- 1/2 cucumber, diced
- 1/4 cup olive oil
- 2 tablespoons red wine vinegar
- Salt and pepper to taste

Instructions:

1. In a large bowl, combine chickpeas, spinach, feta, red onion, and cucumber.
2. In a small bowl, whisk together olive oil, red wine vinegar, salt, and pepper.
3. Pour the dressing over the salad and toss to combine. Serve chilled or at room temperature.

Teriyaki Chicken Stir-Fry

Ingredients:

- 1 pound boneless chicken breast, sliced
- 2 cups mixed vegetables (broccoli, bell peppers, carrots)
- 1/2 cup teriyaki sauce
- 2 tablespoons sesame oil
- 3 cloves garlic, minced
- Cooked rice or noodles for serving

Instructions:

1. In a large skillet or wok, heat sesame oil over medium-high heat. Add sliced chicken and cook until browned, about 5-7 minutes.
2. Add garlic and mixed vegetables, stirring frequently until the vegetables are tender, about 3-5 minutes.
3. Pour teriyaki sauce over the chicken and vegetables, cooking for another 2 minutes until heated through.
4. Serve over cooked rice or noodles.

Mediterranean Couscous Salad

Ingredients:

- 1 cup couscous
- 1 1/4 cups boiling water
- 1 cup cherry tomatoes, halved
- 1/2 cucumber, diced
- 1/4 cup red onion, diced
- 1/2 cup Kalamata olives, sliced
- 1/2 cup feta cheese, crumbled
- 1/4 cup olive oil
- 2 tablespoons red wine vinegar
- Salt and pepper to taste

Instructions:

1. In a bowl, combine couscous and boiling water. Cover and let sit for 5 minutes, then fluff with a fork.
2. In a large bowl, combine couscous, cherry tomatoes, cucumber, red onion, olives, and feta cheese.
3. In a small bowl, whisk together olive oil, red wine vinegar, salt, and pepper.
4. Pour the dressing over the salad and toss to combine. Serve chilled or at room temperature.

Beef and Broccoli Stir-Fry

Ingredients:

- 1 pound flank steak, sliced thinly
- 2 cups broccoli florets
- 3 cloves garlic, minced
- 1 tablespoon ginger, minced
- 1/4 cup soy sauce
- 2 tablespoons oyster sauce
- 1 tablespoon cornstarch
- 2 tablespoons vegetable oil
- Cooked rice for serving

Instructions:

1. In a bowl, mix soy sauce, oyster sauce, and cornstarch. Add sliced beef and marinate for 15 minutes.
2. In a large skillet or wok, heat vegetable oil over medium-high heat. Add garlic and ginger, sautéing until fragrant.
3. Add the marinated beef and stir-fry for 3-4 minutes until browned.
4. Add broccoli and a splash of water, covering the pan for 2-3 minutes until broccoli is tender.
5. Serve hot over cooked rice.

Shrimp Tacos with Cabbage Slaw

Ingredients:

- 1 pound shrimp, peeled and deveined
- 1 tablespoon olive oil
- 1 teaspoon chili powder
- Salt and pepper to taste
- 8 small corn tortillas
- 2 cups green cabbage, shredded
- 1/4 cup cilantro, chopped
- Juice of 1 lime

Instructions:

1. In a bowl, toss shrimp with olive oil, chili powder, salt, and pepper.
2. Heat a skillet over medium heat and cook shrimp for 2-3 minutes on each side until pink and cooked through.
3. In a separate bowl, combine cabbage, cilantro, lime juice, salt, and pepper.
4. To assemble, place shrimp on tortillas and top with cabbage slaw.

Sweet Potato and Black Bean Bowls

Ingredients:

- 2 medium sweet potatoes, diced
- 1 can (15 oz) black beans, drained and rinsed
- 1 teaspoon cumin
- 1 teaspoon paprika
- 2 tablespoons olive oil
- Salt and pepper to taste
- 1 avocado, sliced
- Fresh cilantro for garnish

Instructions:

1. Preheat the oven to 400°F (200°C). Toss diced sweet potatoes with olive oil, cumin, paprika, salt, and pepper. Spread on a baking sheet.
2. Roast sweet potatoes for 25-30 minutes until tender.
3. In a bowl, combine roasted sweet potatoes, black beans, avocado, and cilantro. Serve warm.

Greek Chicken with Tzatziki Sauce

Ingredients:

- 4 boneless chicken breasts
- 1 tablespoon olive oil
- 2 teaspoons oregano
- Salt and pepper to taste
- 1 cup Greek yogurt
- 1 cucumber, grated
- 2 cloves garlic, minced
- Juice of 1 lemon

Instructions:

1. Preheat the grill to medium heat. Season chicken with olive oil, oregano, salt, and pepper.
2. Grill chicken for 6-7 minutes on each side until cooked through.
3. In a bowl, mix Greek yogurt, grated cucumber, garlic, lemon juice, salt, and pepper to make tzatziki.
4. Serve grilled chicken with tzatziki sauce on the side.

Zucchini Noodles with Pesto Chicken

Ingredients:

- 2 large zucchinis, spiralized
- 2 boneless chicken breasts, cooked and shredded
- 1/2 cup pesto sauce
- 1 tablespoon olive oil
- Cherry tomatoes for garnish
- Parmesan cheese for serving

Instructions:

1. In a skillet, heat olive oil over medium heat. Add spiralized zucchini and sauté for 3-4 minutes until tender.
2. Stir in shredded chicken and pesto, cooking until heated through.
3. Serve garnished with cherry tomatoes and Parmesan cheese.

Lentil and Vegetable Soup

Ingredients:

- 1 cup lentils, rinsed
- 1 onion, diced
- 2 carrots, diced
- 2 celery stalks, diced
- 3 cloves garlic, minced
- 6 cups vegetable broth
- 1 teaspoon thyme
- Salt and pepper to taste

Instructions:

1. In a large pot, sauté onion, carrots, celery, and garlic until softened.
2. Add lentils, vegetable broth, thyme, salt, and pepper. Bring to a boil, then reduce heat and simmer for 25-30 minutes until lentils are tender.
3. Serve hot.

Egg Muffins with Spinach and Cheese

Ingredients:

- 6 large eggs
- 1 cup fresh spinach, chopped
- 1/2 cup shredded cheese (cheddar or feta)
- Salt and pepper to taste
- Optional: diced bell peppers or onions

Instructions:

1. Preheat the oven to 350°F (175°C). Grease a muffin tin.
2. In a bowl, whisk together eggs, spinach, cheese, salt, and pepper.
3. Pour the egg mixture evenly into the muffin tin, filling each cup about 3/4 full.
4. Bake for 18-20 minutes until the muffins are set. Let cool slightly before removing from the tin.

BBQ Pulled Pork with Coleslaw

Ingredients:

- 2 pounds pork shoulder
- 1 cup BBQ sauce
- 1 onion, sliced
- 1 cup chicken broth
- Salt and pepper to taste
- 4 hamburger buns
- 2 cups coleslaw mix
- 1/4 cup mayonnaise
- 1 tablespoon apple cider vinegar

Instructions:

1. Season the pork shoulder with salt and pepper and place it in a slow cooker. Top with sliced onion and pour chicken broth over it.
2. Cook on low for 8 hours or until the pork is tender. Shred the pork and mix it with BBQ sauce.
3. In a bowl, combine coleslaw mix, mayonnaise, apple cider vinegar, salt, and pepper.
4. Serve pulled pork on hamburger buns topped with coleslaw.

Asian Peanut Chicken Salad

Ingredients:

- 2 boneless chicken breasts, grilled and sliced
- 4 cups mixed greens
- 1 cup shredded carrots
- 1 bell pepper, sliced
- 1/4 cup chopped peanuts
- 1/4 cup green onions, sliced
- 1/4 cup peanut butter
- 2 tablespoons soy sauce
- 1 tablespoon honey
- Juice of 1 lime

Instructions:

1. In a bowl, whisk together peanut butter, soy sauce, honey, and lime juice to make the dressing.
2. In a large salad bowl, combine mixed greens, carrots, bell pepper, grilled chicken, peanuts, and green onions.
3. Drizzle the dressing over the salad and toss to combine.

Cauliflower Fried Rice

Ingredients:

- 1 head cauliflower, grated into rice-sized pieces
- 2 tablespoons vegetable oil
- 2 eggs, beaten
- 1 cup mixed vegetables (peas, carrots, corn)
- 3 cloves garlic, minced
- 2 tablespoons soy sauce
- Green onions for garnish

Instructions:

1. Heat vegetable oil in a large skillet over medium heat. Add garlic and cook for 1 minute.
2. Push garlic to one side of the skillet and pour in beaten eggs, scrambling until fully cooked.
3. Add cauliflower rice and mixed vegetables, stir-frying for 5-7 minutes.
4. Stir in soy sauce and cook for an additional 2 minutes. Garnish with green onions before serving.

Spicy Chickpea and Quinoa Bowl

Ingredients:

- 1 can (15 oz) chickpeas, drained and rinsed
- 1 cup quinoa, cooked
- 1 tablespoon olive oil
- 1 teaspoon smoked paprika
- 1/2 teaspoon cayenne pepper
- Salt and pepper to taste
- 1 avocado, sliced
- Fresh cilantro for garnish

Instructions:

1. In a skillet, heat olive oil over medium heat. Add chickpeas, smoked paprika, cayenne pepper, salt, and pepper. Cook until chickpeas are heated through and slightly crispy, about 5-7 minutes.
2. In a bowl, combine cooked quinoa and seasoned chickpeas. Top with avocado slices and garnish with fresh cilantro.

Lemon Herb Roasted Chicken Thighs

Ingredients:

- 4 chicken thighs, bone-in and skin-on
- 2 tablespoons olive oil
- Juice of 1 lemon
- 3 cloves garlic, minced
- 1 teaspoon dried thyme
- 1 teaspoon dried rosemary
- Salt and pepper to taste

Instructions:

1. Preheat the oven to 425°F (220°C).
2. In a bowl, mix olive oil, lemon juice, garlic, thyme, rosemary, salt, and pepper.
3. Rub the mixture all over the chicken thighs and place them in a baking dish.
4. Roast for 35-40 minutes or until the chicken is cooked through and the skin is crispy.

Taco Meal Prep with Ground Beef

Ingredients:

- 1 pound ground beef
- 1 packet taco seasoning
- 1 cup diced tomatoes
- 1 cup black beans, drained and rinsed
- 1 cup corn
- 4 meal prep containers
- Optional toppings: shredded cheese, lettuce, salsa

Instructions:

1. In a skillet, brown the ground beef over medium heat. Drain excess fat.
2. Add taco seasoning, diced tomatoes, black beans, and corn. Cook until heated through, about 5 minutes.
3. Divide the mixture into meal prep containers. Add optional toppings as desired.

Grilled Veggie and Hummus Wraps

Ingredients:

- 4 whole wheat tortillas
- 1 zucchini, sliced
- 1 bell pepper, sliced
- 1 cup mushrooms, sliced
- 1 cup hummus
- 1 tablespoon olive oil
- Salt and pepper to taste

Instructions:

1. Preheat the grill or grill pan over medium heat. Toss sliced vegetables with olive oil, salt, and pepper.
2. Grill vegetables for about 5-7 minutes until tender.
3. Spread hummus on each tortilla and top with grilled veggies. Roll up the tortillas and serve.

Overnight Oats with Berries and Almonds

Ingredients:

- 1 cup rolled oats
- 2 cups almond milk (or milk of choice)
- 1/2 cup Greek yogurt
- 1 cup mixed berries (strawberries, blueberries, raspberries)
- 1/4 cup sliced almonds
- 2 tablespoons honey or maple syrup
- 1 teaspoon vanilla extract

Instructions:

1. In a bowl, mix rolled oats, almond milk, Greek yogurt, honey, and vanilla extract until well combined.
2. Divide the mixture into jars or containers. Top each with mixed berries and sliced almonds.
3. Cover and refrigerate overnight. Serve cold in the morning.

Curried Chicken Salad with Apples

Ingredients:

- 2 cups cooked chicken, shredded
- 1/2 cup Greek yogurt
- 1/4 cup mayonnaise
- 1 tablespoon curry powder
- 1 apple, diced
- 1/4 cup raisins
- 1/4 cup chopped walnuts
- Salt and pepper to taste

Instructions:

1. In a large bowl, combine Greek yogurt, mayonnaise, curry powder, salt, and pepper.
2. Add shredded chicken, diced apple, raisins, and walnuts. Mix well to combine.
3. Serve on lettuce leaves or as a sandwich filling.

Spinach and Feta Stuffed Chicken

Ingredients:

- 4 boneless chicken breasts
- 2 cups fresh spinach, chopped
- 1/2 cup feta cheese, crumbled
- 2 cloves garlic, minced
- 1 tablespoon olive oil
- Salt and pepper to taste
- Toothpicks or kitchen twine

Instructions:

1. Preheat the oven to 375°F (190°C).
2. In a skillet, heat olive oil over medium heat. Add garlic and spinach, cooking until wilted.
3. Remove from heat and stir in feta cheese, salt, and pepper.
4. Cut a pocket into each chicken breast and fill with the spinach mixture. Secure with toothpicks or twine.
5. Place stuffed chicken in a baking dish and bake for 25-30 minutes until cooked through.

Meatballs with Zucchini Noodles

Ingredients:

- 1 pound ground beef or turkey
- 1/2 cup breadcrumbs
- 1/4 cup grated Parmesan cheese
- 1 egg
- 2 cloves garlic, minced
- 1 teaspoon Italian seasoning
- 4 zucchinis, spiralized
- 2 cups marinara sauce

Instructions:

1. Preheat the oven to 400°F (200°C).
2. In a bowl, combine ground meat, breadcrumbs, Parmesan cheese, egg, garlic, Italian seasoning, salt, and pepper. Mix well.
3. Form mixture into meatballs and place on a baking sheet. Bake for 20-25 minutes until cooked through.
4. In a skillet, heat marinara sauce and add spiralized zucchini, cooking for 2-3 minutes until tender.
5. Serve meatballs on top of zucchini noodles with additional sauce if desired.

Quinoa and Black Bean Burrito Bowls

Ingredients:

- 1 cup quinoa, cooked
- 1 can (15 oz) black beans, drained and rinsed
- 1 cup corn
- 1 bell pepper, diced
- 1 avocado, diced
- 1/4 cup chopped cilantro
- Juice of 1 lime
- 1 teaspoon cumin
- Salt and pepper to taste

Instructions:

1. In a large bowl, combine cooked quinoa, black beans, corn, bell pepper, avocado, cilantro, lime juice, cumin, salt, and pepper.
2. Mix gently to combine.
3. Serve in bowls, garnished with additional cilantro and lime wedges if desired.

Beef and Sweet Potato Skillet

Ingredients:

- 1 pound ground beef
- 2 medium sweet potatoes, diced
- 1 onion, diced
- 2 cloves garlic, minced
- 1 teaspoon paprika
- 1 teaspoon cumin
- Salt and pepper to taste
- Fresh parsley for garnish

Instructions:

1. In a large skillet, brown ground beef over medium heat. Drain excess fat.
2. Add diced onion and garlic, cooking until softened.
3. Stir in diced sweet potatoes, paprika, cumin, salt, and pepper. Cover and cook for 15-20 minutes until sweet potatoes are tender, stirring occasionally.
4. Garnish with fresh parsley before serving.

Caprese Pasta Salad

Ingredients:

- 12 oz pasta (fusilli or penne)
- 1 cup cherry tomatoes, halved
- 1 cup mozzarella balls, halved
- 1/4 cup fresh basil, chopped
- 1/4 cup olive oil
- 2 tablespoons balsamic vinegar
- Salt and pepper to taste

Instructions:

1. Cook pasta according to package instructions. Drain and rinse under cold water.
2. In a large bowl, combine cooked pasta, cherry tomatoes, mozzarella balls, and basil.
3. In a small bowl, whisk together olive oil, balsamic vinegar, salt, and pepper.
4. Drizzle dressing over the pasta salad and toss to combine. Serve chilled or at room temperature.

Chickpea and Spinach Stew

Ingredients:

- 1 can (15 oz) chickpeas, drained and rinsed
- 4 cups fresh spinach
- 1 onion, diced
- 2 cloves garlic, minced
- 1 can (14 oz) diced tomatoes
- 1 teaspoon cumin
- 1 teaspoon paprika
- Salt and pepper to taste
- Olive oil for cooking
  Instructions:

1. In a large pot, heat olive oil over medium heat. Add diced onion and garlic, cooking until softened.
2. Stir in cumin and paprika, cooking for 1 minute until fragrant.
3. Add chickpeas, diced tomatoes, and spinach, stirring to combine. Cook until spinach is wilted, about 5 minutes.
4. Season with salt and pepper to taste and serve warm.

Grilled Shrimp with Mango Salsa

Ingredients:

- 1 pound shrimp, peeled and deveined
- 1 tablespoon olive oil
- Salt and pepper to taste
- 1 mango, diced
- 1/2 red onion, diced
- 1/2 red bell pepper, diced
- Juice of 1 lime
- Fresh cilantro for garnish

Instructions:

1. Preheat the grill to medium-high heat. Toss shrimp with olive oil, salt, and pepper.
2. Grill shrimp for 2-3 minutes per side until cooked through.
3. In a bowl, combine diced mango, red onion, red bell pepper, lime juice, and cilantro.
4. Serve grilled shrimp topped with mango salsa.

Chicken Fajita Meal Prep Bowls

Ingredients:

- 1 pound chicken breast, sliced
- 1 bell pepper, sliced
- 1 onion, sliced
- 1 tablespoon olive oil
- 1 tablespoon fajita seasoning
- 2 cups cooked rice or quinoa
- Optional toppings: avocado, salsa, cheese

Instructions:

1. In a skillet, heat olive oil over medium heat. Add chicken, bell pepper, onion, and fajita seasoning. Cook until chicken is cooked through and veggies are tender.
2. Divide cooked rice or quinoa into meal prep containers.
3. Top with chicken and veggie mixture. Add optional toppings as desired.

Sweet and Spicy Chicken Drumsticks

Ingredients:

- 2 pounds chicken drumsticks
- 1/4 cup honey
- 1/4 cup soy sauce
- 1 tablespoon sriracha (adjust to taste)
- 2 cloves garlic, minced
- Salt and pepper to taste

Instructions:

1. Preheat the oven to 400°F (200°C).
2. In a bowl, whisk together honey, soy sauce, sriracha, garlic, salt, and pepper.
3. Place drumsticks in a baking dish and pour sauce over them, coating evenly.
4. Bake for 30-35 minutes or until chicken is cooked through and caramelized.

Baked Tilapia with Lemon and Herbs

Ingredients:

- 4 tilapia fillets
- 2 tablespoons olive oil
- Juice of 1 lemon
- 1 teaspoon dried oregano
- 1 teaspoon garlic powder
- Salt and pepper to taste

Instructions:

1. Preheat the oven to 375°F (190°C).
2. Place tilapia fillets on a baking sheet lined with parchment paper.
3. Drizzle olive oil and lemon juice over the fillets. Sprinkle with oregano, garlic powder, salt, and pepper.
4. Bake for 15-20 minutes or until fish flakes easily with a fork.

Ratatouille with Quinoa

Ingredients:

- 1 zucchini, diced
- 1 eggplant, diced
- 1 bell pepper, diced
- 1 onion, diced
- 2 cups diced tomatoes (canned or fresh)
- 2 cloves garlic, minced
- 1 teaspoon dried thyme
- 1 cup quinoa, cooked
- Olive oil for cooking
- Salt and pepper to taste

Instructions:

1. In a large skillet, heat olive oil over medium heat. Add onion and garlic, cooking until softened.
2. Add zucchini, eggplant, and bell pepper. Cook for about 5-7 minutes until tender.
3. Stir in diced tomatoes, thyme, salt, and pepper. Simmer for 10 minutes.
4. Serve ratatouille over cooked quinoa.

Thai Red Curry with Vegetables

Ingredients:

- 1 tablespoon coconut oil
- 1 onion, diced
- 2 cloves garlic, minced
- 1 tablespoon ginger, minced
- 1 can (14 oz) coconut milk
- 2 tablespoons red curry paste
- 2 cups mixed vegetables (bell peppers, carrots, broccoli)
- 1 cup vegetable broth
- 1 tablespoon soy sauce
- Fresh basil for garnish

Instructions:

1. In a large pot, heat coconut oil over medium heat. Add onion, garlic, and ginger, cooking until fragrant.
2. Stir in red curry paste and cook for 1-2 minutes.
3. Add coconut milk, vegetable broth, and mixed vegetables. Bring to a simmer and cook for 10-15 minutes until vegetables are tender.
4. Stir in soy sauce and garnish with fresh basil before serving.

Greek Turkey Burgers with Tzatziki

Ingredients:

- 1 pound ground turkey
- 1/4 cup feta cheese, crumbled
- 1/4 cup chopped parsley
- 1 teaspoon garlic powder
- Salt and pepper to taste
- 4 whole wheat burger buns
- For the tzatziki:
    - 1 cup Greek yogurt
    - 1/2 cucumber, grated and drained
    - 1 clove garlic, minced
    - 1 tablespoon lemon juice
    - Salt and pepper to taste

Instructions:

1. In a bowl, combine ground turkey, feta cheese, parsley, garlic powder, salt, and pepper. Form into 4 patties.
2. Grill or cook patties in a skillet over medium heat for 5-7 minutes on each side or until cooked through.
3. For the tzatziki, mix together Greek yogurt, grated cucumber, garlic, lemon juice, salt, and pepper in a bowl.
4. Serve turkey burgers on whole wheat buns topped with tzatziki.

Pesto Chicken and Veggie Skewers

Ingredients:

- 1 pound chicken breast, cut into cubes
- 2 cups mixed vegetables (zucchini, bell peppers, cherry tomatoes)
- 1/4 cup pesto sauce
- Salt and pepper to taste
- Skewers (wooden or metal)

Instructions:

1. Preheat the grill to medium-high heat.
2. In a bowl, combine chicken cubes, mixed vegetables, pesto, salt, and pepper. Toss to coat.
3. Thread chicken and vegetables onto skewers.
4. Grill skewers for 10-15 minutes, turning occasionally, until chicken is cooked through.

Miso-Glazed Eggplant

Ingredients:

- 2 medium eggplants, sliced in half lengthwise
- 1/4 cup miso paste (white or red)
- 2 tablespoons mirin
- 2 tablespoons honey or maple syrup
- 1 tablespoon sesame oil
- 2 tablespoons soy sauce
- Sesame seeds for garnish
- Green onions, chopped for garnish

Instructions:

1. Preheat the oven to 400°F (200°C). Line a baking sheet with parchment paper.
2. In a bowl, whisk together the miso paste, mirin, honey, sesame oil, and soy sauce until smooth.
3. Place the eggplant halves cut-side up on the baking sheet. Brush the miso glaze generously over the cut sides.
4. Roast the eggplant in the preheated oven for 25-30 minutes, or until tender and caramelized.
5. Remove from the oven and garnish with sesame seeds and chopped green onions before serving.

Creamy Tuscan Chicken

Ingredients:

- 1 pound chicken breast, seasoned with salt and pepper
- 2 tablespoons olive oil
- 2 cups spinach
- 1/2 cup sun-dried tomatoes, chopped
- 1 cup heavy cream
- 1/2 cup grated Parmesan cheese
- 1 teaspoon Italian seasoning

Instructions:

1. In a skillet, heat olive oil over medium heat. Add chicken and cook until golden brown on both sides. Remove and set aside.
2. In the same skillet, add spinach and sun-dried tomatoes, cooking until spinach is wilted.
3. Stir in heavy cream, Parmesan cheese, and Italian seasoning. Return chicken to the skillet and simmer until cooked through.

Breakfast Burrito Bowls

Ingredients:

- 1 cup cooked brown rice or quinoa
- 4 eggs, scrambled
- 1/2 cup black beans, drained and rinsed
- 1/2 avocado, sliced
- 1/2 cup salsa
- Fresh cilantro for garnish
- Salt and pepper to taste

Instructions:

1. In a bowl, layer cooked rice or quinoa as the base.
2. Top with scrambled eggs, black beans, avocado, and salsa.
3. Season with salt and pepper and garnish with fresh cilantro before serving.

Black Bean and Corn Salad

Ingredients:

- 1 can (15 oz) black beans, drained and rinsed
- 1 cup corn (fresh, frozen, or canned)
- 1 bell pepper, diced
- 1/2 red onion, diced
- 1/4 cup fresh cilantro, chopped
- Juice of 1 lime
- Salt and pepper to taste

Instructions:

1. In a large bowl, combine black beans, corn, bell pepper, red onion, and cilantro.
2. Drizzle with lime juice and season with salt and pepper.
3. Toss to combine and serve chilled or at room temperature.

Roasted Vegetable and Quinoa Salad

Ingredients:

- 1 cup quinoa, rinsed
- 2 cups vegetable broth
- 2 cups mixed vegetables (bell peppers, zucchini, carrots)
- 2 tablespoons olive oil
- Salt and pepper to taste
- 1/4 cup feta cheese (optional)
- 1/4 cup fresh parsley, chopped

Instructions:

1. Preheat the oven to 400°F (200°C). Toss mixed vegetables with olive oil, salt, and pepper, then spread on a baking sheet. Roast for 20-25 minutes.
2. Meanwhile, cook quinoa in vegetable broth according to package instructions.
3. In a large bowl, combine cooked quinoa, roasted vegetables, feta cheese, and parsley. Toss to combine and serve warm or at room temperature.

Chicken Alfredo with Broccoli

Ingredients:

- 8 oz fettuccine pasta
- 1 pound chicken breast, sliced
- 2 cups broccoli florets
- 1 cup heavy cream
- 1/2 cup grated Parmesan cheese
- 2 tablespoons olive oil
- Salt and pepper to taste

Instructions:

1. Cook fettuccine according to package instructions, adding broccoli in the last 2-3 minutes of cooking.
2. In a skillet, heat olive oil over medium heat. Add sliced chicken, seasoning with salt and pepper, and cook until browned and cooked through.
3. Reduce heat, then stir in heavy cream and Parmesan cheese, cooking until thickened.
4. Drain pasta and broccoli, then combine with the chicken Alfredo sauce.

Teriyaki Tofu with Mixed Vegetables

Ingredients:

- 1 block firm tofu, pressed and cubed
- 2 cups mixed vegetables (broccoli, bell peppers, carrots)
- 1/4 cup teriyaki sauce
- 2 tablespoons olive oil
- Sesame seeds for garnish

Instructions:

1. In a skillet, heat olive oil over medium heat. Add cubed tofu and cook until golden brown on all sides.
2. Add mixed vegetables to the skillet and stir-fry until tender.
3. Pour teriyaki sauce over tofu and vegetables, cooking for an additional 2-3 minutes.
4. Garnish with sesame seeds and serve warm.

Pasta Primavera with Chicken

Ingredients:

- 8 oz pasta (penne or rotini)
- 1 pound chicken breast, sliced
- 2 cups mixed vegetables (zucchini, bell peppers, asparagus)
- 2 tablespoons olive oil
- 1/2 teaspoon Italian seasoning
- Salt and pepper to taste

Instructions:

1. Cook pasta according to package instructions.
2. In a skillet, heat olive oil over medium heat. Add sliced chicken and cook until browned.
3. Add mixed vegetables and Italian seasoning, cooking until vegetables are tender.
4. Toss cooked pasta with chicken and vegetables, seasoning with salt and pepper.

Lemon Garlic Shrimp with Broccoli

Ingredients:

- 1 pound shrimp, peeled and deveined
- 2 cups broccoli florets
- 3 cloves garlic, minced
- Juice of 1 lemon
- 2 tablespoons olive oil
- Salt and pepper to taste

Instructions:

1. In a skillet, heat olive oil over medium heat. Add minced garlic and cook until fragrant.
2. Add shrimp and cook until pink and cooked through.
3. Stir in broccoli and lemon juice, cooking until broccoli is tender. Season with salt and pepper before serving.

Caprese Stuffed Portobello Mushrooms

Ingredients:

- 4 large portobello mushrooms, stems removed
- 1 cup cherry tomatoes, halved
- 1 cup mozzarella balls, halved
- 1/4 cup fresh basil, chopped
- 2 tablespoons balsamic glaze
- Olive oil for drizzling
- Salt and pepper to taste

Instructions:

1. Preheat the oven to 375°F (190°C).
2. Place portobello mushrooms on a baking sheet and drizzle with olive oil, salt, and pepper.
3. In a bowl, combine cherry tomatoes, mozzarella, and basil. Spoon mixture into each mushroom cap.
4. Bake for 15-20 minutes until mushrooms are tender. Drizzle with balsamic glaze before serving.

Chili Lime Grilled Chicken

Ingredients:

- 1 pound chicken breast
- Juice of 2 limes
- 2 tablespoons olive oil
- 1 tablespoon chili powder
- Salt and pepper to taste

Instructions:

1. In a bowl, mix lime juice, olive oil, chili powder, salt, and pepper. Add chicken and marinate for at least 30 minutes.
2. Preheat the grill to medium-high heat. Grill chicken for 6-7 minutes per side or until cooked through.
3. Let rest for a few minutes before slicing and serving.

Vegetable Stir-Fry with Brown Rice

Ingredients:

- 2 cups mixed vegetables (carrots, bell peppers, broccoli)
- 2 tablespoons soy sauce
- 2 tablespoons olive oil
- 2 cloves garlic, minced
- 2 cups cooked brown rice
- Sesame seeds for garnish

Instructions:

1. In a skillet, heat olive oil over medium heat. Add minced garlic and mixed vegetables, stir-frying until tender.
2. Stir in soy sauce and cook for an additional minute.
3. Serve stir-fried vegetables over cooked brown rice and garnish with sesame seeds.

Baked Ziti with Spinach and Ricotta

Ingredients:

- 12 oz ziti pasta
- 2 cups marinara sauce
- 1 cup ricotta cheese
- 2 cups fresh spinach, chopped
- 1 cup shredded mozzarella cheese
- 1/2 cup grated Parmesan cheese
- 1 teaspoon Italian seasoning
- Salt and pepper to taste

Instructions:

1. Preheat the oven to 375°F (190°C). Cook ziti pasta according to package instructions; drain and set aside.
2. In a large bowl, mix together marinara sauce, ricotta cheese, spinach, Italian seasoning, salt, and pepper.
3. Combine cooked ziti with the sauce mixture, then transfer to a greased baking dish.
4. Top with mozzarella and Parmesan cheese.
5. Bake for 25-30 minutes until the cheese is bubbly and golden.

Spaghetti Squash with Turkey Meat Sauce

Ingredients:

- 1 medium spaghetti squash
- 1 lb ground turkey
- 1 cup marinara sauce
- 1 small onion, chopped
- 2 cloves garlic, minced
- 1 teaspoon Italian seasoning
- Salt and pepper to taste
- Olive oil for cooking

Instructions:

1. Preheat the oven to 400°F (200°C). Cut spaghetti squash in half and scoop out seeds. Drizzle with olive oil, season with salt and pepper, and place cut-side down on a baking sheet. Roast for 30-40 minutes until tender.
2. In a skillet, heat olive oil over medium heat. Add onion and garlic; sauté until softened.
3. Add ground turkey, cooking until browned. Stir in marinara sauce and Italian seasoning; simmer for 10 minutes.
4. Once squash is cooked, scrape the insides with a fork to create spaghetti-like strands. Serve topped with turkey meat sauce.